A Sad

Say the words. Listen for the **sho**

back	cat	fast	hand	man
nap	rag	sad	tag	wax

Read the clues. Write the correct words.

1. This is at the end of your arm. ____________________
2. This is the opposite of *happy.* ____________________
3. Candles are made from this. ____________________
4. This is the opposite of *front.* ____________________
5. A boy grows up to be this. ____________________
6. This is a game kids play. ____________________
7. This means *quick*. ____________________
8. This is a small piece of cloth. ____________________
9. This can be a pet. ____________________
10. This means *a short sleep.* ____________________

A Wet Pen

Say the words. Listen for the **short e** sound as in *pen.*

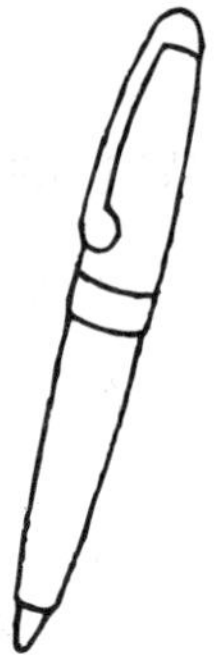

bed	end	fed	get	next
pen	sent	test	wet	yes

Read the clues. Write the words to complete the puzzle.

1. Jake got _____ in the rain.
2. The dog has not been _____ yet.
3. The opposite of *no* is _____.
4. You can write with a _____.
5. A _____ is a place to sleep.
6. I liked the _____ of that book.
7. Did you _____ that for your birthday?
8. I'll see you _____ week.
9. Eve _____ a card to her friend.
10. Did you study for the _____?

1.			t	
2.	f			
3.		e		
4.			n	
5.	b			
6.		n		
7.			t	
8.			x	
9.		e		
10.			s	

Zip It Up

Say the words. Listen for the **short i** sound as in *zip.*

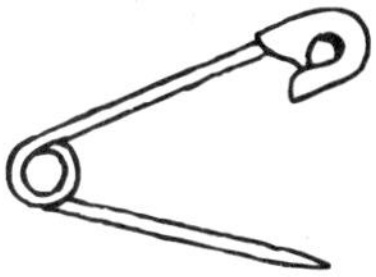

bib	fix	is	
it	kick	kid	pin
sick	wig	zip	

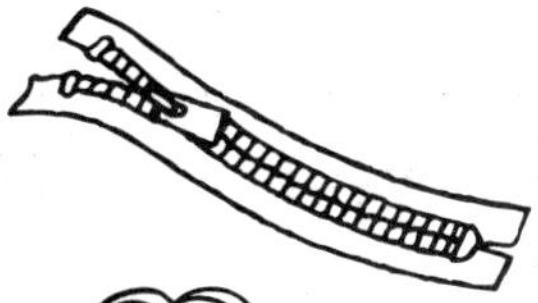

Use the code to figure out the words.

a	b	c	d	e	f	g	h	i	j	k	l	m
1	2	3	4	5	6	7	8	9	10	11	12	13
n	o	p	q	r	s	t	u	v	w	x	y	z
14	15	16	17	18	19	20	21	22	23	24	25	26

1. ___ ___ ___
   23 9 7

2. ___ ___ ___
   16 9 14

3. ___ ___ ___
   2 9 2

4. ___ ___ ___
   26 9 16

5. ___ ___ ___ ___
   19 9 3 11

6. ___ ___ ___
   11 9 4

7. ___ ___ ___
   6 9 24

8. ___ ___
   9 20

9. ___ ___
   9 19

10. ___ ___ ___ ___
   11 9 3 11

Fox Sings a Song

Say the words. Listen for the **short o** sound as in *fox.*

cost	fox	hot	job	lock
mop	nod	on	pond	song

Find and circle the words in the puzzle.
The words go across and down.

a	r	h	o	t	k	b	l	f	n	o	b	s
n	m	o	a	x	o	l	d	g	o	n	w	j
c	o	z	x	y	c	o	s	t	d	i	v	o
b	p	f	o	x	g	c	m	c	e	j	d	b
p	o	n	d	h	t	k	e	s	o	n	g	u

Change the first letter in each word to make a list word.

1. long ____________
2. lost ____________
3. top ____________
4. sock ____________
5. fond ____________
6. box ____________
7. got ____________
8. in ____________
9. sob ____________
10. rod ____________

Duck in the Tub

Say the words. Listen for the **short u** sound as in *tub.*

club	duck	hug	jump	mud
nut	run	tub	up	us

Write the words in the puzzle. Use the pictures to help you.

1. 

2. 

3. 

4. 

5. 

6. 

7. 

8. 

9. 

10. 

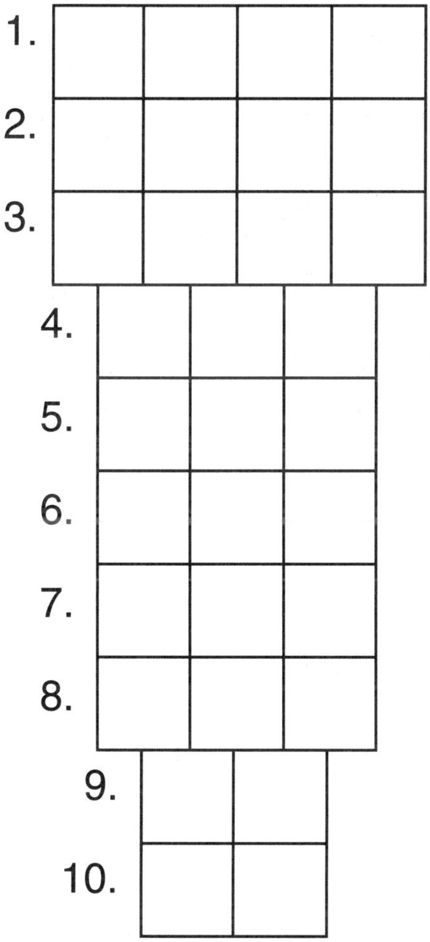

Short Vowels

Write the missing short vowel: **a**, **e**, **i**, **o**, or **u**.

1.  c___t 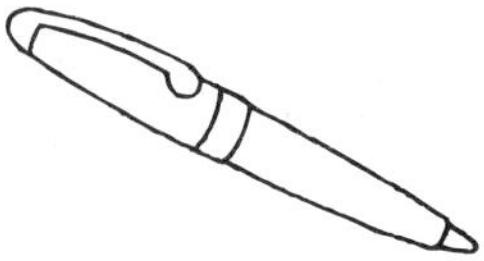 p___n

2.  f___x  d___ck

3.  m___d  b___d

4.  m___n  b___b

5.  w___t  w___g

6. 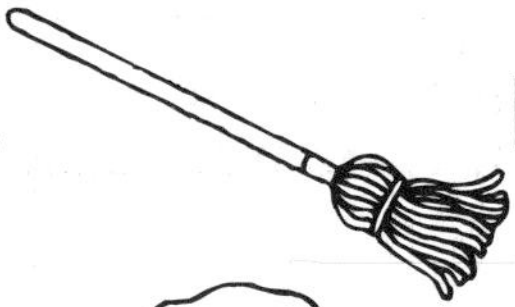 m___p  p___nd

7.  n___t  k___ck

8.  h___nd  l___ck

Let's Play

Say the words. Listen for the **long a** sound as in *bake, rain,* and *day.*

bake	day	grade	late	paint
play	rain	say	tail	wait

Read the clues. Write the words in the puzzle.

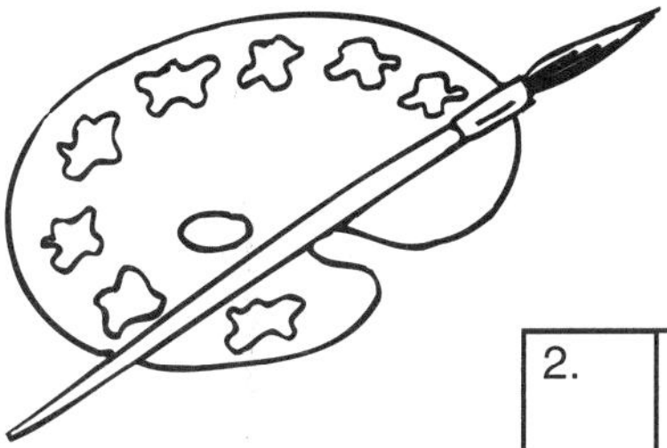

Down

1. What a beautiful _____!
2. I like to _____ pictures.
3. What _____ are you in?
5. What did she _____?
7. I was _____ for school.

Across

2. Would you like to _____ outside?
4. We played in the _____ and got wet.
6. Our dog wags his _____ when he's happy.
8. Did you _____ that chocolate cake?
9. Sometimes it's hard to _____ for a turn.

Meet the Team

Say the words. Listen for the **long e** sound as in *heat* and *keep.*

clean	heat	read	sea	team
green	keep	meet	sleep	week

Follow the signs. Add and subtract letters to make words.

1. bus – bu + ea = ________________
2. grape – ape + een = ________________
3. pot – po + eam = ________________
4. cling – ing + ean = ________________
5. sled – d + ep = ________________
6. she – s + at = ________________
7. shore – sho + ad = ________________
8. rake – ra + ep = ________________
9. crow – cro + eek = ________________
10. time – ti + et = ________________

Find the Word

Say the words. Listen for the **long i** sound as in *wild, kind,* and *time.*

mild	wild	find	grind	kind
mind	five	prize	slide	time

Use the code to figure out the words.

1. ■ ● ✳ ❤ ______________________
2. ✚ ● ✳ ❤ ______________________
3. ❁ ● ▼ ❤ ______________________
4. ✕ ▲ ● ❑ ➔ ______________________
5. ◆ ▲ ● ✳ ❤ ______________________
6. ❖ ▼ ● ❤ ➔ ______________________
7. ✓ ● ✱ ➔ ______________________
8. ✚ ● ▼ ❤ ______________________
9. ✓ ● ✳ ❤ ______________________
10. ★ ● ✚ ➔ ______________________

❤ = d
➔ = e
✓ = f
◆ = g
● = i
■ = k
▼ = l
✚ = m
✳ = n
✕ = p
▲ = r
❖ = s
★ = t
✱ = v
❁ = w
❑ = z

Snow at Home

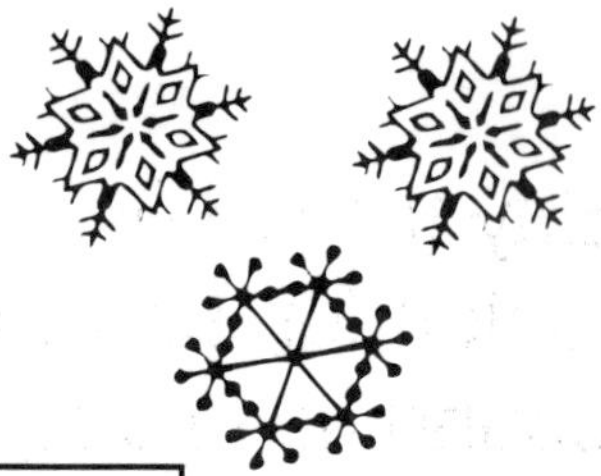

Say the words. Listen for the **long o** sound as in *go, coat, old, grow,* and *home.*

go	coat	load	old	sold
grow	snow	home	note	rope

Write each word in the correct word shape.

1.

2.

3.

4.

5.

6.

7.

8.

9.

10.

Use the Clues

Say the words.
Listen for the **long u** sound as in *use, blue,* and *fruit.*

cute rule tune
use blue due glue
true fruit suit

Look at the pictures. Complete the sentences.

1. I used _____________ to fix the torn paper.

2. Do you remember the safety _____________?

3. Let's hum that _____________ again.

4. The sky is _____________.

5. Dad wore his new _____________ to work.

6. When is the report _____________?

7. That puppy is so _____________!

8. May I _____________ your scissors?

9. Apples are my favorite _____________.

10. Everything he said was _____________.

Long Vowels

Write the missing long vowel: **a**, **e**, **i**, **o**, or **u**.

1.  c____at	2.  gl____e	3.  sl____ep
4.  t____il	5.  f____ve	6.  sn____w
7.  r____in	8.  fr____it	9.  h____me
10.  pr____ze	11.  w____ek	12.  sl____de

Lots of Blends

Say the words. Listen for the two sounds that begin each word as in *black* and *sled.*

	black	clean	clap
flag	flip	globe	plant
	plug	sled	slide

Read the clues. Write the words.

1. It begins like  and ends like  . ________________
2. It begins like  and ends like  . ________________
3. It begins like  and ends like  . ________________
4. It begins like  and ends like  . ________________
5. It begins like  and ends like  . ________________
6. It begins like  and ends like  . ________________
7. It begins like  and ends like  . ________________
8. It begins like  and ends like  . ________________
9. It begins like  and ends like  . ________________
10. It begins like  and ends like  . ________________

A Barrel of Blends

Say the words. Listen for the two sounds that begin each word as in *crab* and *free.*

brave	bride	crab	
crate	drip	free	grab
prune	trip	trust	

Write the correct word to finish each sentence.

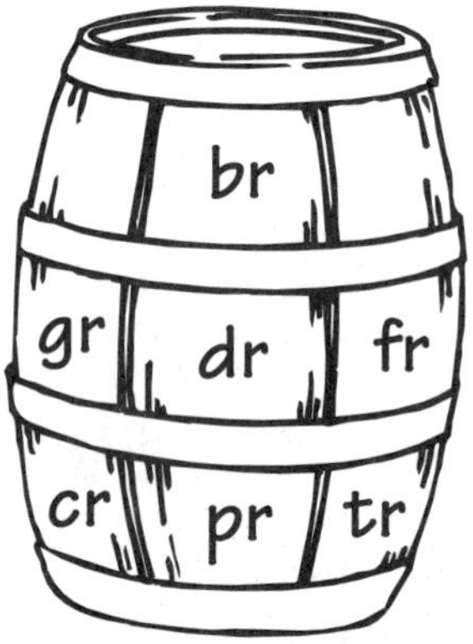

1. A _____________ is a dried plum.
2. I _____________ you to be on time.
3. That _____________ is full of oranges.
4. The _____________ looked beautiful in white.
5. We won _____________ tickets to the concert.
6. She went on a _____________ to visit her grandmother.
7. Water will _____________ if the pipe is broken.
8. I had to _____________ a quick bite because I was late.
9. The _____________ fireman went in the burning house.
10. A _____________ has a hard shell and lives in the water.

Spot or Stop?

Say the words. Listen for the two sounds that begin each word as in *skin* and *smile.*

skin	skunk	smell	smile	snack
snap	spot	stop	store	swing

Write the word that rhymes with each picture.

1. 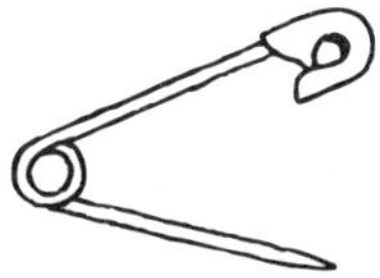 ____________

2.  ____________

3.  ____________

4.  ____________

5.  ____________

6.  ____________

7.  ____________

8.  ____________

9.  ____________

10.  ____________

Blends Review

Circle the correct spelling of each word.

1.		clap	klap	clape
2.		flog	frag	flag
3.		krab	crab	cabe
4.		bride	brid	breod
5.		sope	stop	stope
6.		scunc	sknuk	skunk
7.	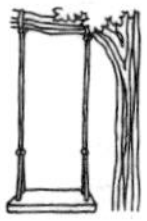	swinn	swing	sine
8.		smale	smll	smile
9.		glob	gloob	globe
10.	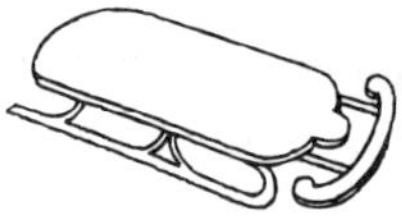	sled	sleed	slede

Write It Right

Say the words. Sometimes the same two consonant letters spell one ending sound as in *kiss* and *doll.*

add	odd		class
grass	kiss	bell	doll
well	egg		buzz

Circle the misspelled word in each sentence. Write it correctly.

1. That dlol looks like a real baby. ____________________
2. How many kids are in your ssalc? ____________________
3. The green gsars grew very tall. ____________________
4. My dog gave me a wet siks. ____________________
5. A bee makes a bzzu sound. ____________________
6. I had a fried geg for breakfast. ____________________
7. I know how to dda numbers. ____________________
8. He does ddo jobs after school. ____________________
9. A blel makes a ringing sound. ____________________
10. You can get water from a llew. ____________________

What Luck?

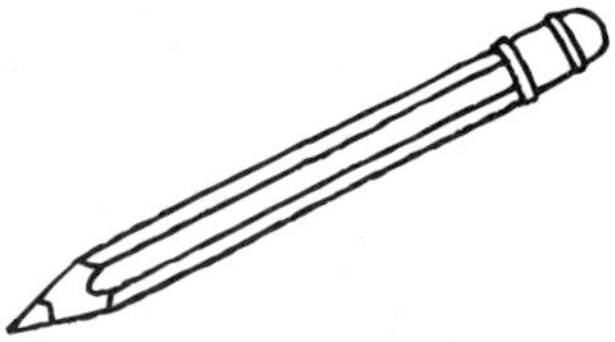

Say the words. Listen for the sound that the letters **ck** make as in *rock* and *truck.*

stack	neck	kick	pick	sick
clock	rock	duck	luck	truck

Write the word that answers each question.

1. What word begins like  ? ____________________
2. What word begins like 

? ____________________
3. What word begins like 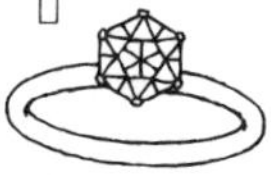 ? ____________________
4. What word begins like  ? ____________________
5. What word begins like 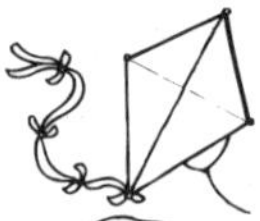 ? ____________________
6. What word begins like  ? ____________________
7. What word begins like  ? ____________________
8. What word begins like  ? ____________________
9. What word begins like  ? ____________________
10. What word begins like  ? ____________________

How Does It End?

Say the words. Listen for the two sounds that end each word as in *ask, gasp,* and *best.*

ask	lisp
desk	best
mask	last
risk	must
gasp	past

Read the clues. Write the words in the puzzle.

Across

2. He speaks with a _____ .
4. You can sit at a _____ to write.
5. We watched a movie _____ night.
8. A _____ covered his face.
9. The bus drove right _____ us.

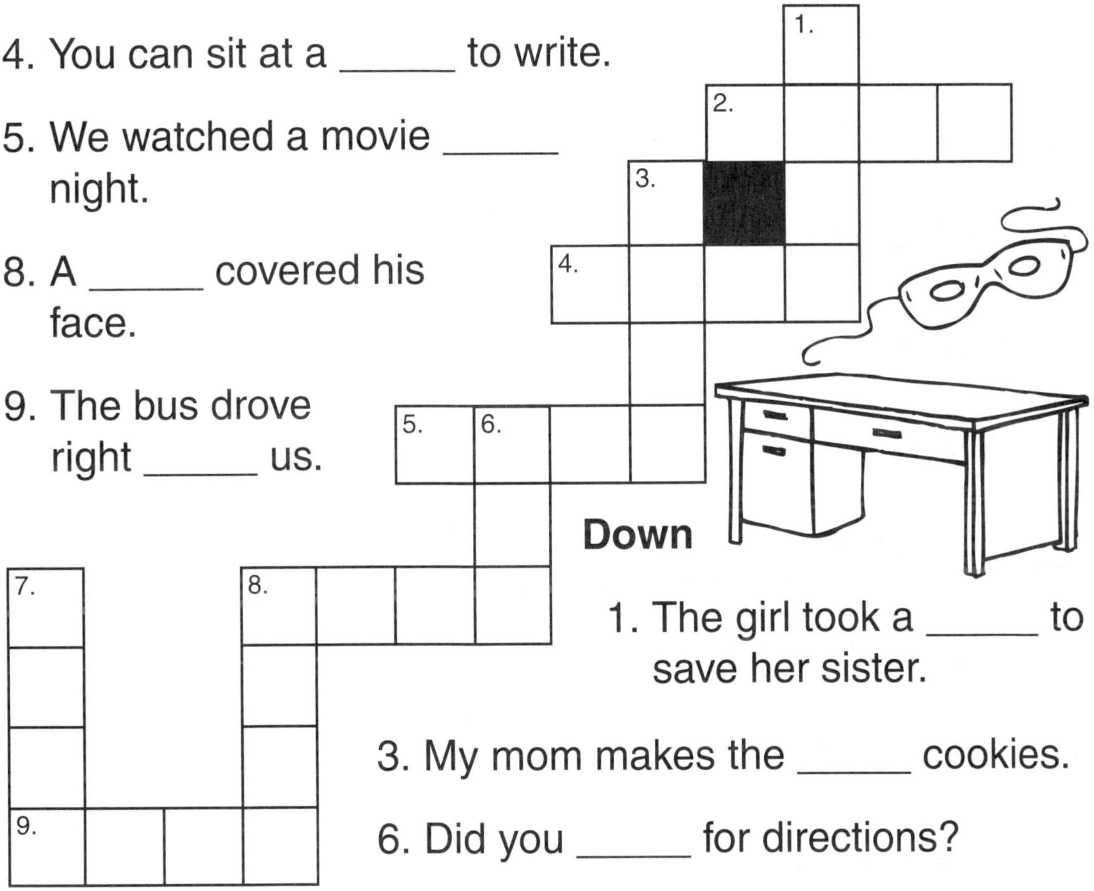

Down

1. The girl took a _____ to save her sister.
3. My mom makes the _____ cookies.
6. Did you _____ for directions?
7. I heard a _____ from the scared boy.
8. You _____ eat to live.

It's in the Bank

Say the words. Listen for the two sounds that end each word as in *and, ink,* and *tent.*

and	band	end	mend	bank
ink	sank	tent	hint	sent

Unscramble the letters. Write the words correctly.

1. ndem ____________
2. dna ____________
3. bkan ____________
4. setn ____________
5. kin ____________
6. bnda ____________
7. ksan ____________
8. dne ____________
9. tten ____________
10. hnit ____________

Find and circle the words in the puzzle. The words go across and down.

a	n	d	b	d	f	e	n	d
t	e	n	t	b	c	k	e	l
s	s	n	r	a	m	s	h	b
m	e	n	d	n	g	a	i	a
o	n	i	j	k	h	n	n	n
p	t	i	n	k	q	k	t	d

Use the Code

Say the words. Listen for the two sounds that end each word as in *golf, film, help,* and *melt.*

golf	self		elm
film	help	gulp	belt
felt	melt		tilt

Use the code to figure out the words.

b	e	f	g	h	i	l	m	o	p	s	t	u
1	2	3	4	5	6	7	8	9	10	11	12	13

1. 5 + 2 + 7 + 10 ____________________
2. 11 + 2 + 7 + 3 ____________________
3. 8 + 2 + 7 + 12 ____________________
4. 12 + 6 + 7 + 12 ____________________
5. 1 + 2 + 7 + 12 ____________________

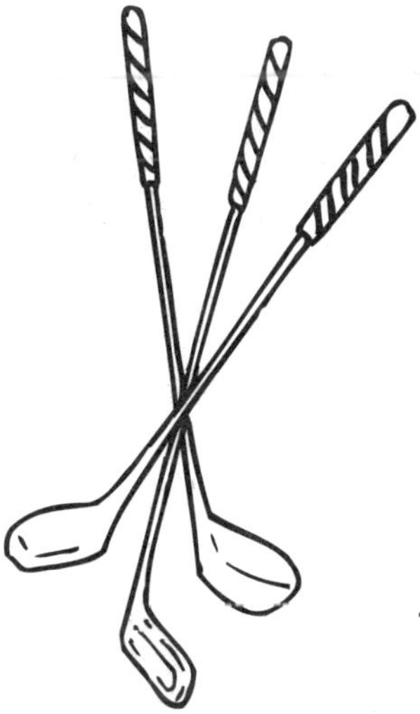

6. 2 + 7 + 8 ____________________
7. 4 + 9 + 7 + 3 ____________________
8. 3 + 6 + 7 + 8 ____________________
9. 4 + 13 + 7 + 10 ____________________
10. 3 + 2 + 7 + 12 ____________________

Spelling Checkup

Fill in the bubbles to choose the correct spelling of each word.

1.	○ grss	○ grass	○ jrass	
2.	○ truck	○ trukc	○ rukt	
3.	○ deks	○ dkss	○ desk	
4.	○ tent	○ tetn	○ teent	
5.	○ glof	○ goolf	○ golf	
6.	○ belt	○ blet	○ btel	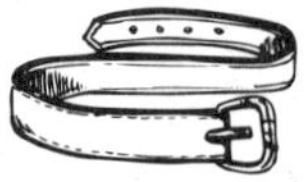
7.	○ ikn	○ inkk	○ ink	
8.	○ clock	○ klock	○ clicke	
9.	○ ege	○ eeg	○ egg	
10.	○ dkuc	○ duck	○ dukc	

This or That?

Say the words. The letters **sh** spell one sound as in *shop.* The letters **th** spell one sound as in *math.*

she	shine		shop
wish	wash	that	the
this	math		with

Write **sh** or **th** to finish the words in the sentences. Then draw a line to match each sentence to its picture.

1. My favorite subject is ma_____.

2. The stars _____ine at night.

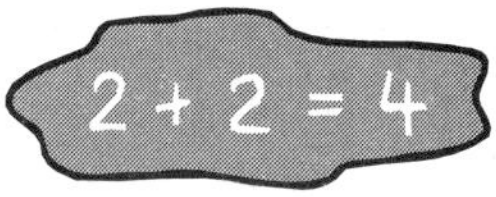

3. Please shut _____e door.

4. Is _____is your jacket?

5. We saw kittens at the pet _____op.

6. Let's wa_____ our hands before lunch.

7. I made a wi_____ on my birthday.

8. Is _____e going to read a book?

9. He stayed up so late _____at he was tired.

10. I went to the mall wi_____ my mom.

Where or When?

Say the words. The letters **ch** spell one sound as in *much.*
The letters **wh** spell one sound as in *white.*

change	cheap	cheese	much	beach
what	wheel	when	where	white

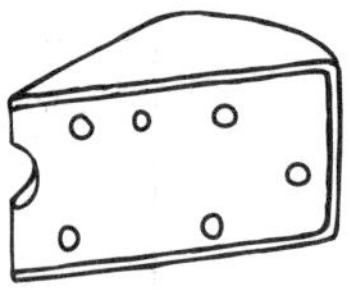

Write each word in the correct word shape.

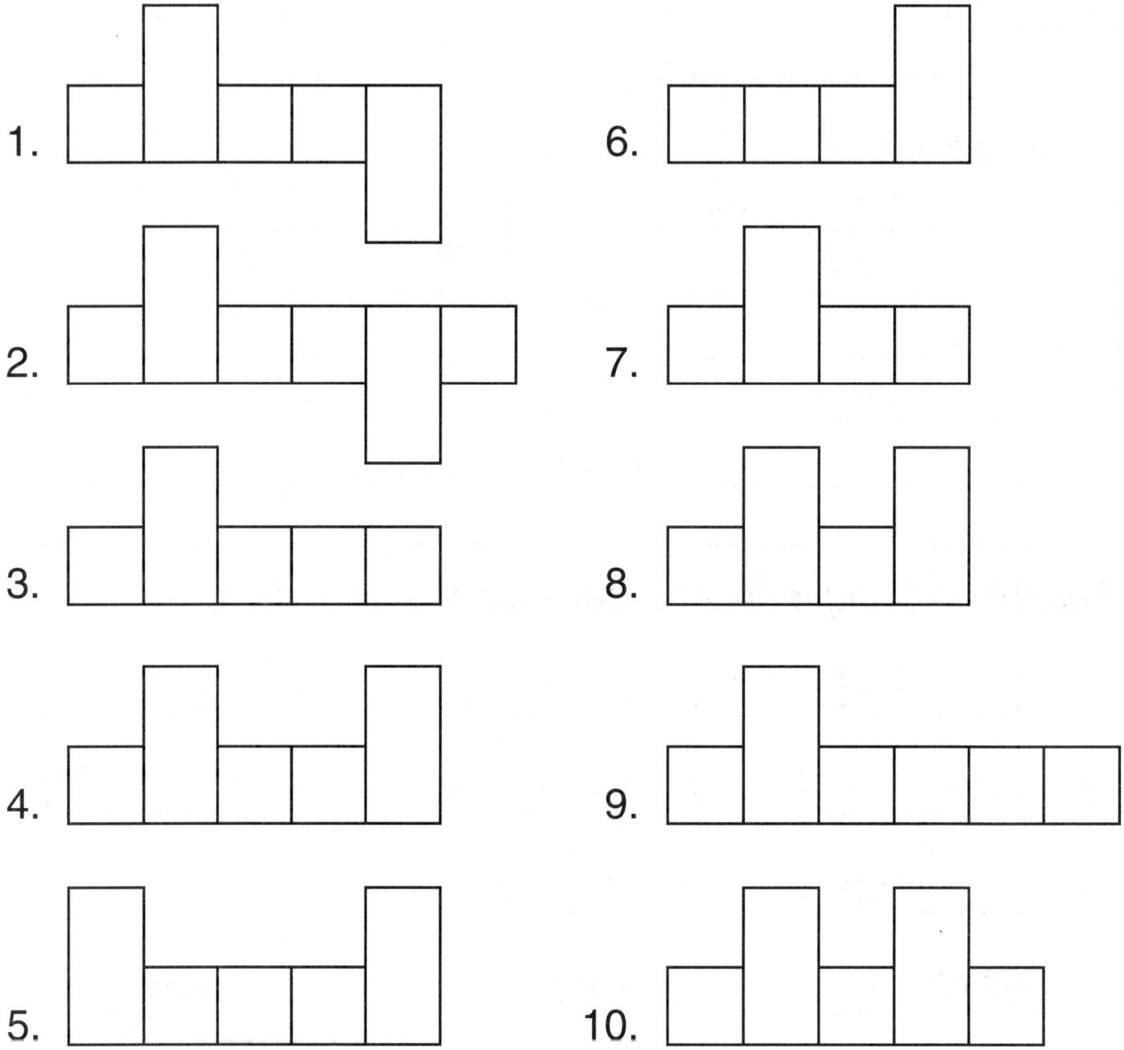

Foot or Food?

Say the words. The letters **oo** can stand for two different sounds, as in *foot* or *food.*

book	cool	food	foot	good
room	shook	stood	soon	tooth

Write each word in the correct box to show the sound that **oo** stands for.

oo as in *moon*

____
____
____
____
____

oo as in *wood*

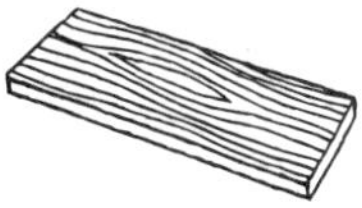

____
____
____
____
____

Add the missing letters to make the words in the box.

1. f_____d
2. bo_____
3. _____om
4. sho_____
5. t_____th
6. co_____
7. f_____t
8. sto_____
9. go_____
10. s_____n

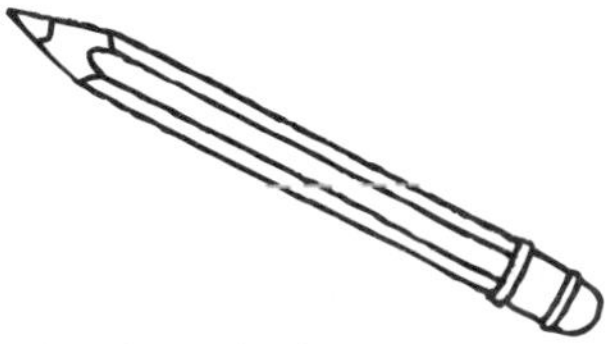

Start the Car

Say the words. Listen for the **ar** sound as in *car* and the **or** sound as in *fork.*

arm	car	dark	hard	start
corn	fork	horse	more	sport

Write the word that answers each question.

1. Which word is the opposite of *less*? ____________
2. Which word describes a physical game? ____________
3. Which word is the opposite of *light*? ____________
4. Which word is the opposite of *easy*? ____________
5. Which word is a yellow vegetable? ____________
6. Which word is a part of the body? ____________
7. Which word is something you drive? ____________
8. Which word is an animal? ____________
9. Which word is something you eat with? ____________
10. Which word means *to begin*? ____________

Pull-Out Answers

Page 1

1. hand
2. sad
3. wax
4. back
5. man
6. tag
7. fast
8. rag
9. cat
10. nap

Page 2

1. wet
2. fed
3. yes
4. pen
5. bed
6. end
7. get
8. next
9. sent
10. test

Page 3

1. wig
2. pin
3. bib
4. zip
5. sick
6. kid
7. fix
8. it
9. is
10. kick

Page 4

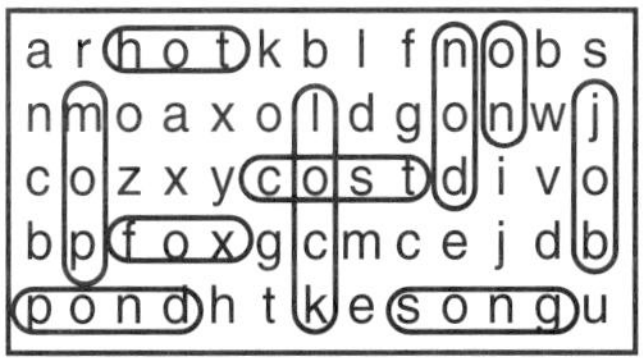

1. song
2. cost
3. mop
4. lock
5. pond
6. fox
7. hot
8. on
9. job
10. nod

Page 5

1. club
2. jump
3. duck
4. tub
5. nut
6. mud
7. hug
8. run
9. us
10. up

Page 6

1. c**a**t, p**e**n
2. f**o**x, d**u**ck
3. m**u**d, b**e**d
4. m**a**n, b**i**b
5. w**e**t, w**i**g
6. m**o**p, p**o**nd
7. n**u**t, k**i**ck
8. h**a**nd, l**o**ck

Page 7

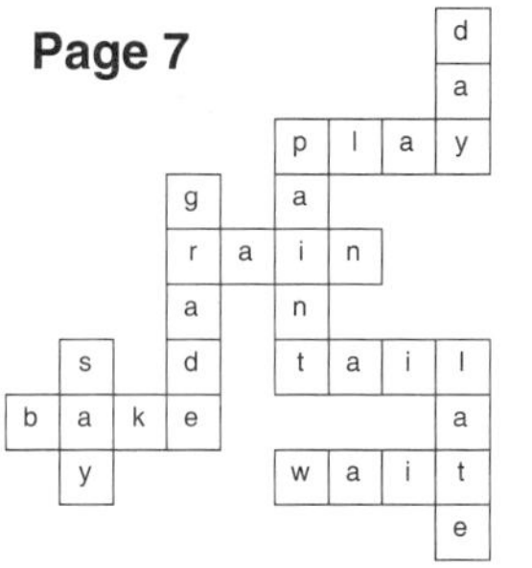

Page 8

1. sea
2. green
3. team
4. clean
5. sleep
6. heat
7. read
8. keep
9. week
10. meet

Page 9

1. kind
2. mind
3. wild
4. prize
5. grind
6. slide
7. five
8. mild
9. find
10. time

Page 10

1. snow
2. old
3. note
4. go
5. coat
6. grow
7. sold
8. load
9. rope
10. home

Page 11

1. glue
2. rule
3. tune
4. blue
5. suit
6. due
7. cute
8. use
9. fruit
10. true

Page 12

1. c**o**at
2. gl**u**e
3. sl**e**ep
4. t**a**il
5. f**i**ve
6. sn**o**w
7. r**a**in
8. fr**u**it
9. h**o**me
10. pr**i**ze
11. w**e**ek
12. sl**i**de

Page 13

1. flag
2. clap
3. globe
4. plant
5. slide
6. black
7. clean
8. flip
9. plug
10. sled

Page 14

1. prune
2. trust
3. crate
4. bride
5. free
6. trip
7. drip
8. grab
9. brave
10. crab

Page 15

1. skin
2. snap
3. skunk
4. smile
5. spot
6. stop
7. smell
8. swing
9. snack
10. store

Pull-Out Answers

Page 16

1. clap
2. flag
3. crab
4. bride
5. stop
6. skunk
7. swing
8. smile
9. globe
10. sled

Page 17

1. circled—dlol
   written—doll
2. circled—ssalc
   written—class
3. circled—gsars
   written—grass
4. circled—siks
   written—kiss
5. circled—bzzu
   written—buzz
6. circled—geg
   written—egg
7. circled—dda
   written—add
8. circled—ddo
   written—odd
9. circled—blel
   written—bell
10. circled—llew
    written—well

Page 18

1. luck
2. stack
3. rock
4. pick
5. kick
6. neck
7. duck
8. sick
9. clock
10. truck

Page 19

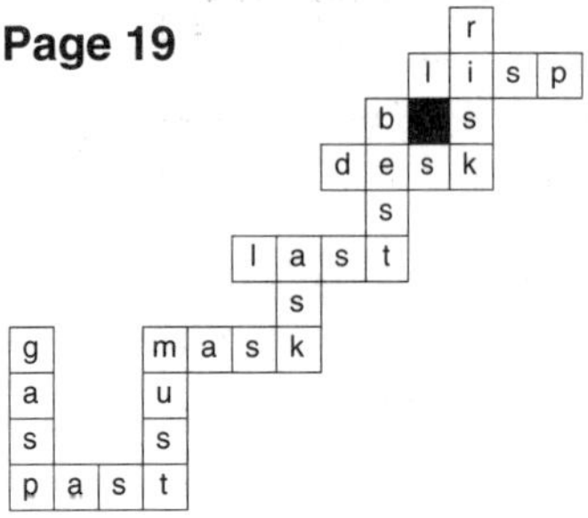

Page 20

1. mend
2. and
3. bank
4. sent
5. ink
6. band
7. sank
8. end
9. tent
10. hint

a	n	d	b	d	f	e	n	d
t	e	n	t	b	c	k	e	l
s	s	n	r	a	m	s	h	b
m	e	n	d	n	g	a	i	a
o	n	i	j	k	h	n	n	n
p	t	i	n	k	q	k	t	d

Page 21

1. help
2. self
3. melt
4. tilt
5. belt
6. elm
7. golf
8. film
9. gulp
10. felt

Page 22

1. grass
2. truck
3. desk
4. tent
5. golf
6. belt
7. ink
8. clock
9. egg
10. duck

Page 23

1. ma**th**
2. **sh**ine
3. **th**e
4. **th**is
5. **sh**op
6. wa**sh**
7. wi**sh**
8. **sh**e
9. **th**at
10. wi**th**

Page 24

1. cheap
2. change
3. where
4. wheel
5. beach
6. much
7. when
8. what
9. cheese
10. white

Page 25

oo as in *moon*	**oo as in *wood***
cool	book
food	foot
room	good
soon	shook
tooth	stood

1. f**oo**d
2. b**oo**k
3. r**oo**m
4. sh**oo**k
5. t**oo**th
6. c**oo**l
7. f**oo**t
8. st**oo**d
9. g**oo**d
10. s**oo**n

Page 26

1. more
2. sport
3. dark
4. hard
5. corn
6. arm
7. car
8. horse
9. fork
10. start

Page 27

sh**ir**t
d**ir**t
t**ur**n
h**er**
sk**ir**t
f**er**n
c**ur**l
g**ir**l
f**ir**st
b**ur**n

Page 28

1. coin
2. point
3. oil
4. boy
5. toy
6. noise
7. join
8. boil
9. joy
10. spoil

Page 29

1. loud
2. how
3. down
4. town
5. owl
6. south
7. proud
8. count
9. growl
10. out

Pull-Out Answers

Page 30
1. draw
2. vault
3. saw
4. fault
5. lawn
6. fraud
7. paw
8. haul
9. pause
10. crawl

Page 31
1. shop
2. beach
3. tooth
4. sport
5. first
6. noise

Page 32

long e	long i
baby	by
crazy	fly
many	shy
only	sky
tiny	try

1. shy
2. by
3. many
4. tiny
5. baby
6. crazy
7. fly
8. sky
9. only
10. try

Page 33
1. boxes
2. dishes
3. kings
4. rugs
5. socks
6. peaches
7. pens
8. glasses
9. bags
10. buses

Page 34
1. packed
2. jumping
3. sleeping
4. meeting
5. locked
6. swinging
7. bumped
8. rolled
9. brushing
10. tossed

Page 35
1. circled—skiped
   written—skipped
2. circled—winer
   written—winner
3. circled—spining
   written—spinning
4. circled—hoter
   written—hotter
5. circled—bigest
   written—biggest
6. circled—runing
   written—running
7. circled—sadest
   written—saddest
8. circled—seting
   written—setting
9. circled—planed
   written—planned
10. circled—stoped
    written—stopped

Page 36
1. waved
2. filing
3. dining
4. hired
5. baked
6. loved
7. hoping
8. liking
9. taped
10. wiping

Page 37
1. cried
2. crazier
3. babies
4. ponies
5. messiest
6. silliest
7. ladies
8. tried
9. luckier
10. funniest

Page 38
1. tri
2. byy
3. dishs
4. bumpd
5. slepping
6. winnnr
7. hardesst
8. bakked
9. likng
10. babees

Page 39

sail**or**
flow**er**
teach**er**
act**or**
coll**ar**
farm**er**
sist**er**
mot**or**
sug**ar**
doct**or**

Page 40
1. bottle
2. riddle
3. table
4. jungle
5. able
6. cable
7. uncle
8. bubble
9. candle
10. puzzle

Page 41

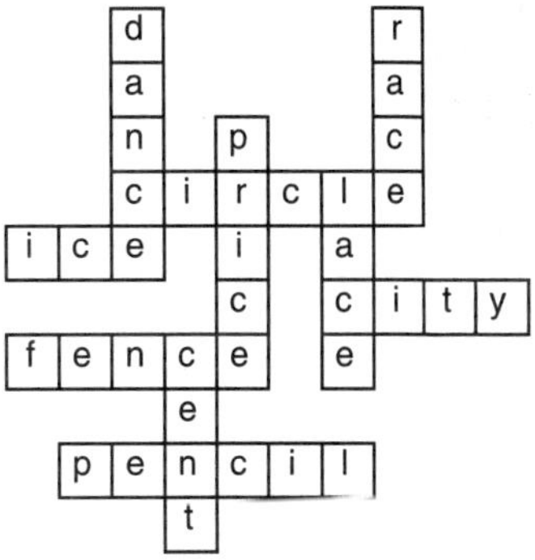

Pull-Out Answers

Page 42

1. wage
2. gem
3. stage
4. gentle
5. sponge
6. change
7. page
8. engine
9. large
10. huge

c	b	h	v	s	t	a	g	e	n	w	g	e	n	t	l	e
g	r	u	u	y	q	l	a	r	g	e	p	e	r	g	a	k
e	c	g	x	p	a	g	e	d	e	n	g	i	n	e	r	m
m	x	e	f	w	a	g	e	c	m	h	j	p	q	n	g	l
c	h	a	n	g	e	v	b	z	a	s	p	o	n	g	e	d

Page 43

1. resolve
2. unsafe
3. recall
4. uneven
5. unlike
6. unfair
7. remake
8. repay
9. refill
10. unkind

Page 44

1. flow**er**
2. doct**or**
3. bubb**le**
4. cand**le**
5. **ce**nt
6. fen**ce**
7. spon**ge**
8. **ge**m
9. bea**ch**
10. **re**fill
11. sail**or**
12. tab**le**

Page 45

1. four, for
2. bee, be
3. two, to
4. blue, blew
5. son, sun

Page 46

1. hear
2. maid
3. sale
4. hour
5. hole
6. made
7. here
8. our
9. whole
10. sail

Page 47

1. can't
2. isn't
3. they'll
4. didn't
5. he'll
6. don't
7. I'll
8. she'll
9. aren't
10. you'll

Page 48

1. I've
2. who's
3. we've
4. it's
5. they're
6. you've
7. she's
8. he's
9. you're
10. we're

Page 49

1. circled—sidein
   written—inside
2. circled—longbe
   written—belong
3. circled—bemay
   written—maybe
4. circled—dayto
   written—today
5. circled—outwith
   written—without
6. circled—selfher
   written—herself
7. circled—selfmy
   written—myself
8. circled—sidebe
   written—beside
9. circled—sideout
   written—outside
10. circled—selfhim
    written—himself

Page 50

1. goldfish
2. raincoat
3. sailboat
4. flagpole
5. bedroom
6. sunshine
7. bookcase
8. pancake
9. doorbell
10. homework

Page 51

1. circled—freind
   written—friend
2. circled—sed
   written—said
3. circled—peopel
   written—people
4. circled—kno
   written—know
5. circled—wons
   written—once
6. circled—agin
   written—again
7. circled—wud
   written—would
8. circled—faverit
   written—favorite
9. circled—becuz
   written—because
10. circled—rong
    written—wrong

Page 52

1. C
2. D
3. A
4. A
5. D
6. A
7. A

It's Your Turn

Say the words. Listen for the **vowel sound with r** as in *her*, *dirt*, and *turn*.

fern		her	dirt
first	girl	shirt	skirt
burn		curl	turn

Write **er**, **ir**, or **ur** to complete each word.

 sh___t	 f___n
 d___t	 c___l
 t___n	 g___l
 h___	 f___st
 sk___t	 b___n

Riddle Fun

Say the words. Listen for the **oi** or **oy** sound as in *coin* and *boy*.

boil	coin	join	noise	oil
point	spoil	boy	joy	toy

Write the word that answers each riddle.

1. You can buy things with me. What am I? __________
2. I am the sharp end of a pencil. What am I? __________
3. I help cars run. What am I? __________
4. I am the opposite of a girl. What am I? __________
5. I can be a ball, a doll, or a top. What am I? __________
6. I am a sound that is loud. What am I? __________
7. This means *to put together.* What is this? __________
8. This can happen to water. What is this? __________
9. This is a strong feeling of happiness.
   What is this? __________
10. This happens if you leave milk out.
    What is this? __________

Out on the Town

Say the words. Listen for the **ou** or **ow** sound as in *out* and *town.*

out	count	loud	proud	south
down	growl	how	owl	town

Follow the signs. Add and subtract letters to make words.

1. ball + oud – bal = ________________
2. house – use + w = ________________
3. good + own – goo = ________________
4. into + wn – in = ________________
5. too + wl – to = ________________

6. bus + outh – bu = ________________
7. map + roud – ma = ________________
8. coin – in + unt = ________________
9. grape – ape + owl = ________________
10. go + ut – g = ________________

Time to Pause

Say the words. Listen for the **au** or **aw** sound as in *pause* and *saw.*

fault	fraud		haul
pause	vault	crawl	draw
lawn	paw		saw

Circle the correct word. Write the word.

1. I like to ______________ with crayons.
(draw, paw)

2. The bank keeps money in a ______________ .
(fault, vault)

3. Dad cut the wood with a ______________ .
(saw, draw)

4. Don't worry, it's not your ______________.
(pause, fault)

5. The yard has a beautiful ______________ .
(lawn, fraud)

6. He was arrested for ______________.
(crawl, fraud)

7. The kitten hurt its front ______________.
(paw, pause)

8. We had to ______________ the bed upstairs.
(lawn, haul)

9. After a ______________, the show continued.
(fault, pause)

10. Babies can ______________ fast.
(crawl, saw)

Spelling Review

Fill in the bubbles to choose the correct spelling of each word.

1. The pet _____ is closed today.

   ❍ shop ❍ shope ❍ shopp

2. Let's go to the _____ this weekend.

   ❍ beash ❍ beach ❍ bech

3. I lost another _____.

   ❍ tooth ❍ toot ❍ tooch

4. My favorite _____ is soccer.

   ❍ spirt ❍ soprt ❍ sport

5. I was the _____ one to arrive at the party.

   ❍ furst ❍ first ❍ firts

6. That _____ is giving me a headache.

   ❍ noise ❍ noiz ❍ niice

Y as a Vowel

Say the words. The letter **y** can make a **long e** sound as in *baby* or a **long i** sound as in *fly.*

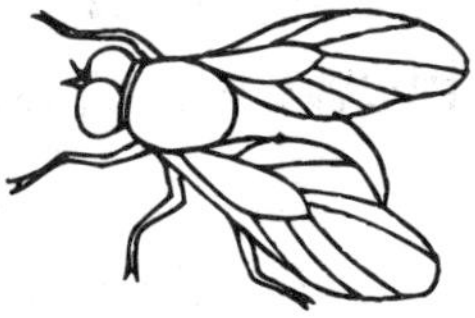

baby	by	crazy	fly	many
only	shy	sky	tiny	try

Write each word in the correct box to show the sound that **y** stands for.

long e	**long i**
______	______
______	______
______	______
______	______
______	______

Unscramble the letters. Write the words correctly.

1. hys ______
2. yb ______
3. yman ______
4. yint ______
5. ybba ______
6. yzarc ______
7. yfl ______
8. syk ______
9. yonl ______
10. ytr ______

Rhyme Time

Say the words. Each word names more than one of something. You add **s** to most words to name more than one. However, you add **es** to words ending in *s, sh, ch,* or *x.*

bags	kings	pens	rugs	socks
boxes	buses	dishes	glasses	peaches

Write the word that rhymes with the boldfaced word in each sentence.

1. The **foxes** are hiding behind the ______________ .
2. Mom **wishes** that we would wash the ______________ .
3. The two ______________ have lots of **rings**.
4. The **bugs** are sleeping on the ______________.
5. Zack's ______________ are full of **rocks**.
6. We went to two **beaches** and ate lots of ______________.
7. I used my ______________ to draw pictures of **hens**.
8. Six kids wear ______________ in the first-grade **classes**.
9. Those ______________ are full of old **rags**.
10. The baby **fusses** when the school ______________ go by.

Word Endings

Say the words. Each word has a root word and an **ed** or **ing** ending.

bumped	locked	packed	rolled	tossed
brushing	jumping	meeting	sleeping	swinging

Look at the picture clues. Write the words in the puzzle.

1. 

2. 

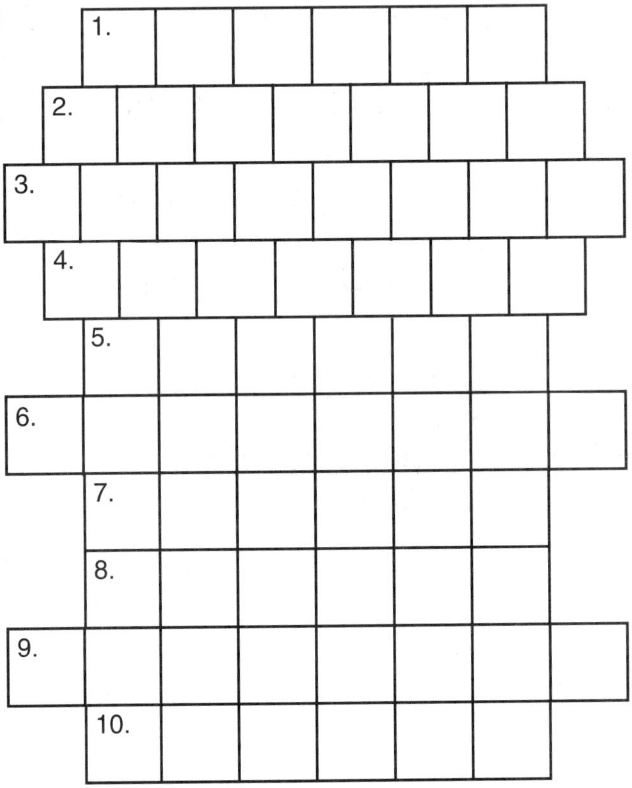

3. 

4. 

5. 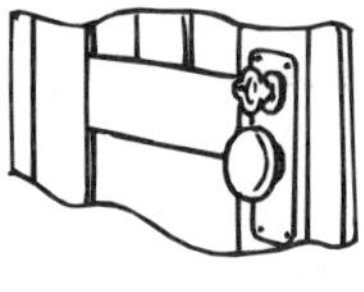

6. 

7. 

8. 

9. 

10. 

Double It

Say the words. Listen for the short vowel sounds. The final consonant in most short vowel words is doubled when the **ed**, **er**, **est**, or **ing** endings are added.

Examples: hop + ed = hopped chop + ing = chopping

planned	skipped	stopped	hotter	winner
biggest	saddest	running	setting	spinning

Circle the misspelled word in each sentence. Write it correctly.

1. I'm hungry because I skiped lunch today. ______________
2. Our class is the winer of the paper drive. ______________
3. That spider is spining a beautiful web. ______________
4. It is hoter today than it was yesterday. ______________
5. Meg has the bigest dog on the block. ______________
6. The horse is runing in a race today. ______________
7. That is the sadest movie I ever saw. ______________
8. Jack is seting the table for dinner. ______________
9. Mom planed a birthday party for me. ______________
10. We stoped for some ice cream. ______________

Drop It

Say the words. Each word is made from a word ending in **silent e**. When a word ends in **silent e**, the **e** is dropped when the **ed** or **ing** endings are added.

Examples: fire + ed = fired   shave + ing = shaving

baked	hired	loved	taped	waved
dining	filing	hoping	liking	wiping

Write the new words. Be sure to follow the spelling rule.

1. wave + ed ____________________
2. file + ing ____________________
3. dine + ing ____________________
4. hire + ed ____________________
5. bake + ed ____________________
6. love + ed ____________________
7. hope + ing ____________________
8. like + ing ____________________
9. tape + ed ____________________
10. wipe + ing ____________________

Adding Endings

Say the words. Each word is made from a word ending in **y**. When a word ends in **y**, the **y** is changed to an **i** when the **ed**, **er**, **es**, or **est** endings are added.

Examples: cherry + es = cherries   lazy + est = laziest

cried	tried	crazier	luckier	babies
ladies	ponies	funniest	messiest	silliest

Write the list word that is made from the root word shown.

1. cry ____________________
2. crazy ____________________
3. baby ____________________
4. pony ____________________
5. messy ____________________
6. silly ____________________
7. lady ____________________
8. try ____________________
9. lucky ____________________
10. funny ____________________

Spell Check

Look at each set of words. Circle the word that is not spelled correctly.

1.	baby	fly	tri	sky
2.	only	tiny	many	byy
3.	boxes	dishs	socks	rugs
4.	bumpd	locked	rolled	tossed
5.	brushing	meeting	slepping	jumping
6.	stopped	hotter	winnnr	skipped
7.	biggest	hardesst	running	spinning
8.	bakked	loved	waved	taped
9.	filing	hoping	likng	wiping
10.	cried	babees	ponies	funniest

Sound Alikes

Say the words. The endings **er**, **or**, and **ar** sound very much alike.

flower	farmer	sister	
teacher	actor	doctor	sailor
motor	collar	sugar	

Write **er**, **or**, or **ar** to complete each word.
Circle the correct picture.

sail____  	farm____  
flow____  	sist____  
teach____  	mot____  
act____  	sug____  
coll____  	doct____  

Mystery Words

Say the words. Listen for the sound **le** makes at the end of each word as in *table* and *bottle.*

able		bottle	bubble
cable	candle	jungle	puzzle
riddle		table	uncle

Use the code to figure out the words.

1. ____ ____ ____ ____ ____ ____
2 11 14 14 9 5

2. ____ ____ ____ ____ ____ ____
13 7 4 4 9 5

3. ____ ____ ____ ____ ____
14 1 2 9 5

4. ____ ____ ____ ____ ____ ____
8 15 10 6 9 5

5. ____ ____ ____ ____
1 2 9 5

6. ____ ____ ____ ____ ____
3 1 2 9 5

7. ____ ____ ____ ____ ____
15 10 3 9 5

8. ____ ____ ____ ____ ____ ____
2 15 2 2 9 5

9. ____ ____ ____ ____ ____ ____
3 1 10 4 9 5

10. ____ ____ ____ ____ ____ ____
12 15 16 16 9 5

a	b	c	d	e	g	i	j
1	2	3	4	5	6	7	8
l	n	o	p	r	t	u	z
9	10	11	12	13	14	15	16

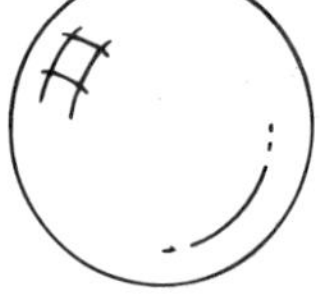

Another Sound for c

Say the words. Listen for the **s** sound that the letter **c** can make as in *city* and *race.*

cent	circle	city	dance	fence
ice	lace	pencil	price	race

Look at the picture clues. Write the words in the puzzle.

Down

1. 

2. 

3. 

5. 

9. 

Across

4. 

6. 

7. 

8. 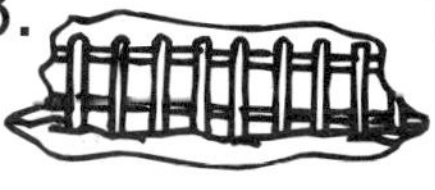

10. 

Another Sound for g

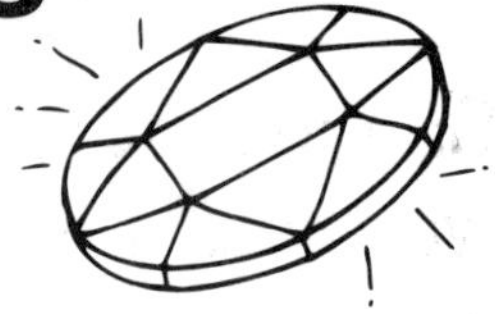

Say the words. Listen for the **j** sound that the letter **g** can make as in *gem* and *page.*

gem	gentle	change	engine	huge
large	page	sponge	stage	wage

Unscramble the letters. Write the words correctly.

1. ewag ________________
2. mge ________________
3. sateg ________________
4. eltnge ________________
5. spgone ________________
6. angech ________________
7. gpea ________________
8. geeinn ________________
9. gerla ________________
10. geuh ________________

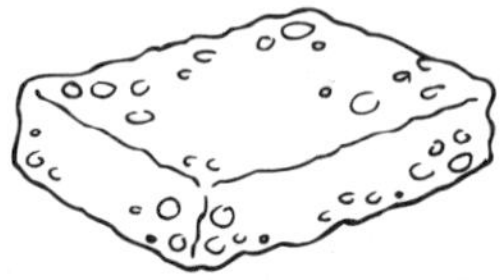

Find and circle the words in the puzzle. The words go across and down.

c	b	h	v	s	t	a	g	e	n	w	g	e	n	t	l	e
g	r	u	u	y	q	l	a	r	g	e	p	e	r	g	a	k
e	c	g	x	p	a	g	e	d	e	n	g	i	n	e	r	m
m	x	e	f	w	a	g	e	c	m	h	j	p	q	n	g	l
c	h	a	n	g	e	v	b	z	a	s	p	o	n	g	e	d

Spelling Prefixes

Say the words. Each root word has a prefix added to the beginning of it. The prefix **un** means *not.* The prefix **re** means *do again.*

uneven	unfair	unkind
unlike	unsafe	
recall	refill	remake
repay	resolve	

Read the clues. Write the words. Circle the prefix in each word.

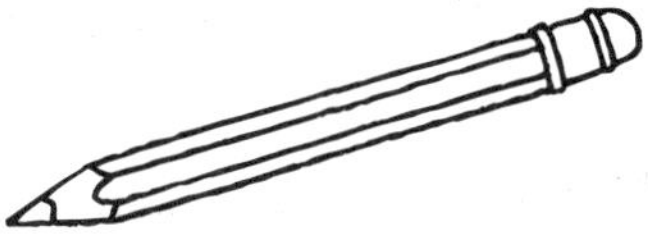

1. This means *to solve again.* ________________
2. This means *not safe.* ________________
3. This means *to call again.* ________________
4. This means *not straight or even.* ________________
5. This means *not like.* ________________
6. This means *not fair.* ________________
7. This means *to make again.* ________________
8. This means *to pay again.* ________________
9. This means *to fill again.* ________________
10. This means *cruel* or *not kind.* ________________

What's Missing?

Write the missing letters to spell the words.

1. 

flow___

2. 

doct___

3. 

bubb___

4. 

cand___

5. 

___nt

6. 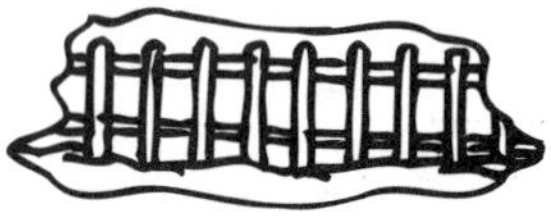

fen___

7. 

spon___

8. 

___em

9. 

bea___

10. 

___fill

11. 

sail___

12. 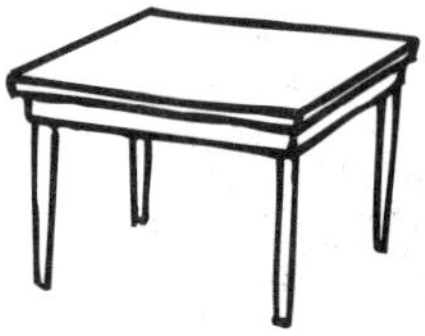

tab___

Be or Bee?

Some words sound the same but have different spellings and meanings. Say the pairs of words on the list.

be	bee
blew	blue
for	four
son	sun
to	two

Look at each pair of words. Write the correct words in the blanks to finish the sentences.

1. These __________ gifts are __________ you.
   (for, four) (for, four)

2. The __________ will __________ at the hive soon.
   (be, bee) (be, bee)

3. My __________ dogs are going __________ the vet.
   (to, two) (to, two)

4. My __________ balloon __________ away.
   (blew, blue) (blew, blue)

5. John's __________ likes to play in the __________.
   (son, sun) (son, sun)

Sounds the Same

hear	here
hole	whole
hour	our
made	maid
sail	sale

Say the pairs of words in the box. Each pair sounds the same but has different meanings.

Write the correct word for each sentence.

1. You use your ears to ________________. (here, hear)
2. The ________________ cleaned the room. (made, maid)
3. I bought these shoes on ________________. (sail, sale)
4. We have to go home in one ________________. (hour, our)
5. I have a ________________ in my sock. (hole, whole)
6. I ________________ a card for my mom. (made, maid)
7. I've been ________________ all day. (here, hear)
8. That is ________________ new house. (hour, our)
9. I ate that ________________ pizza. (hole, whole)
10. A ________________ helps a boat move. (sail, sale)

Spelling Contractions

Say the words. Every word is a contraction. A **contraction** is a word made from two words, but one or more letters are left out. An apostrophe (') takes the place of the missing letters as in *can't* and *I'll.*

aren't	can't	didn't
don't	isn't	
I'll	he'll	she'll
you'll	they'll	

is + not = isn't

Write the contraction for the boldfaced words in each sentence.

1. My baby sister **cannot** walk yet. ________________
2. Ricky **is not** home from school yet. ________________
3. I think **they will** win the contest. ________________
4. I **did not** go to the birthday party. ________________
5. Do you think **he will** find his lost ring? ________________
6. I **do not** like to eat broccoli. ________________
7. **I will** read a new book this week. ________________
8. Beth said **she will** study tonight. ________________
9. We **are not** going to the park today. ________________
10. I hope **you will** visit soon. ________________

More Contractions

Say the words. All the words are contractions.

he's	I've	it's	she's	they're
we're	we've	who's	you're	you've

Write the contraction for each pair of words.

1. I have ____________

2. who is ____________

3. we have ____________

4. it is ____________

5. they are ____________

6. you have ____________

7. she is ____________

8. he is ____________

9. you are ____________

10. we are ____________

Compound Words

Say the words. All the words are compound words. **Compound words** are made by putting two words together. (Example: out + side = outside)

belong	beside	herself	himself	inside
maybe	myself	outside	today	without

Read each sentence. Find and circle the compound word that is not written correctly. Write it correctly.

1. We'll play sidein because of the rain. ________________
2. Does that dog longbe to you? ________________
3. I'm not sure, but bemay you're right. ________________
4. It's Sara's birthday dayto. ________________
5. I won't sleep outwith my teddy bear. ________________
6. The baby walked all by selfher. ________________
7. Sometimes I like to be by selfmy. ________________
8. He sat sidebe his mom. ________________
9. The sideout of our house is blue. ________________
10. Sometimes Bill talks to selfhim. ________________

More Compounds

Say the words. All the words are compound words.

bedroom	bookcase	doorbell	flagpole	goldfish
homework	pancake	raincoat	sailboat	sunshine

Read each sentence. Find and underline two words that can make a compound word. Write the compound word.

1. The gold color of the fish is pretty. ________________
2. I think it will rain so I need my coat. ________________
3. The sail will help the boat move. ________________
4. The school flag is on the pole. ________________
5. Your bed is in your room. ________________
6. I wonder if the sun will shine today. ________________
7. My favorite book is in that case. ________________
8. I used the pan to cook the cake. ________________
9. Open the door when you hear the bell. ________________
10. At home, I have a lot of work to do. ________________

Tricky Words

Say the words. These words are often misspelled because they have tricky spellings.

again	because	favorite	friend	know
once	people	said	would	wrong

Circle the misspelled word in each sentence. Write it correctly.

1. Megan is my best freind.

 ____

2. Ben sed "hello" to me.

 ____

3. How many peopel are coming to the party?

 ____

4. Do you kno how to play chess?

 ____

5. I play soccer wons a week.

 ____

6. Can you play agin?

 ____

7. I wud like to help.

 ____

8. What is your faverit sport?

 ____

9. She took a nap becuz she was tired.

 ____

10. Mom drove down the rong street.

 ____

Find the Mistakes

Fill in the circle under the part of the sentence that contains a misspelled word. If there are no misspelled words, fill in the circle under *None.*

1. I can't | go outside | tody. | None
   Ⓐ Ⓑ Ⓒ Ⓓ

2. The bookcase | is by | the table. | None
   Ⓐ Ⓑ Ⓒ Ⓓ

3. Ouur teacher | made us | a snack. | None
   Ⓐ Ⓑ Ⓒ Ⓓ

4. Maybe they'l | go to | the show. | None
   Ⓐ Ⓑ Ⓒ Ⓓ

5. Her bedroom | is blue | and white. | None
   Ⓐ Ⓑ Ⓒ Ⓓ

6. Her freind | saw the | people dance. | None
   Ⓐ Ⓑ Ⓒ Ⓓ

7. I knoe | you'll wash | the dishes. | None
   Ⓐ Ⓑ Ⓒ Ⓓ